EASY GUITAR

HIGH SCHOOL MUSIC

D1581670

£8
8/
08

2

CONTENTS

ISBN 978-1-4234-3782-6

Walt Disney Music Company
Wonderland Music Company, Inc.

DISTRIBUTED BY

HAL•LEONARD®
CORPORATION
7777 W. BLUEMOUND RD. P.O. BOX 13819 MILWAUKEE, WI 53213

In Australia Contact:
Hal Leonard Australia Pty. Ltd.
4 Lentara Court
Cheltenham, Victoria, 3192 Australia
Email: ausadmin@halleonard.com.au

Visit Hal Leonard Online at
www.halleonard.com

STRUM AND PICK PATTERNS

This chart contains the suggested strum and pick patterns that are referred to by number at the beginning of each song in this book. The symbols ⊓ and ∨ in the strum patterns refer to down and up strokes, respectively. The letters in the pick patterns indicate which right-hand fingers play which strings.

p = **thumb**
i = **index finger**
m = **middle finger**
a = **ring finger**

For example; Pick Pattern 2
is played: thumb - index - middle - ring

Strum Patterns

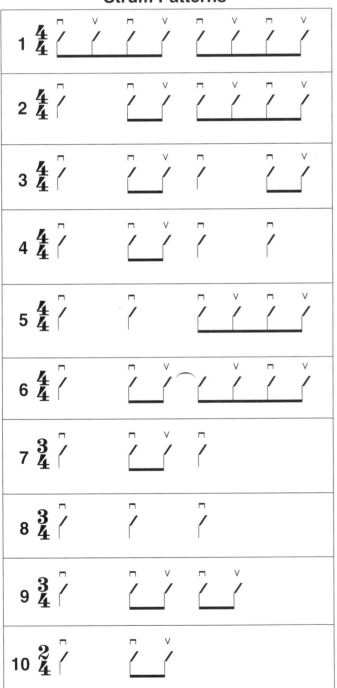

Pick Patterns

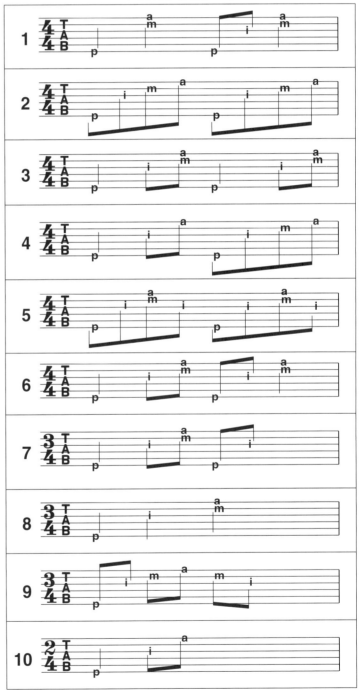

You can use the 3/4 Strum and Pick Patterns in songs written in compound meter (6/8, 9/8, 12/8, etc.). For example, you can accompany a song in 6/8 by playing the 3/4 pattern twice in each measure. The 4/4 Strum and Pick Patterns can be used for songs written in cut time (¢) by doubling the note time values in the patterns. Each pattern would therefore last two measures in cut time.

What Time Is It

Words and Music by Matthew Gerrard and Robbie Nevil

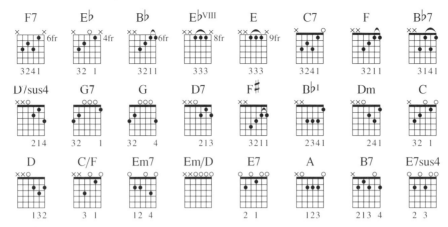

Strum Pattern: 4
Pick Pattern: 1

 Chorus
Moderately fast Funk

Chad: What time is it? __ All: Sum-mer-time. It's our va - ca - tion. Chad: What time is it? __

All: Par - ty time. That's right, say it loud. __ Chad: What time is it? __ All: The time __ of our lives.

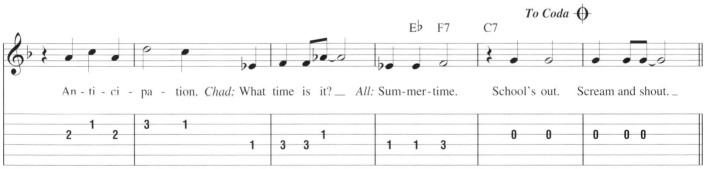

An - ti - ci - pa - tion. Chad: What time is it? __ All: Sum-mer-time. School's out. Scream and shout. __

Verse

1. Troy: Fi - n'ly sum-mer's here. __ Good __ to be chill - in' out. __ I'm off the clock, __ the

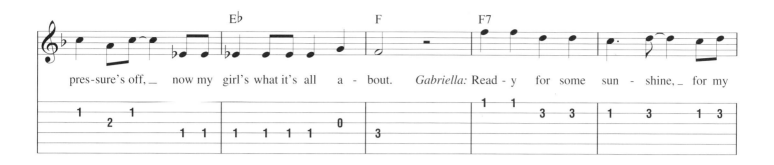

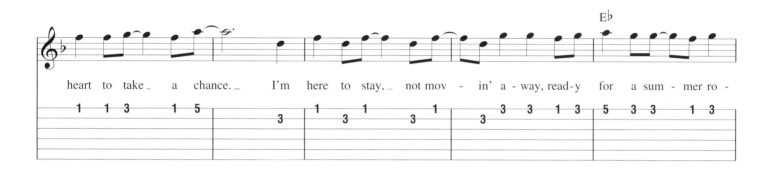

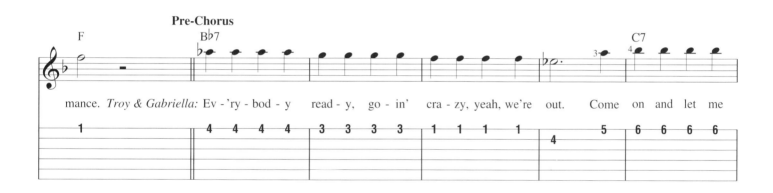

Pre-Chorus

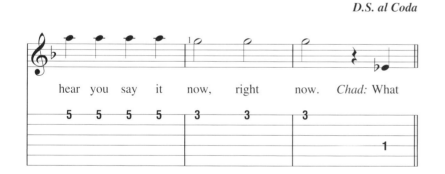 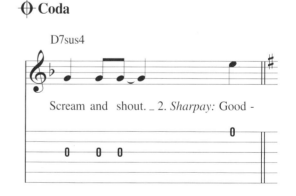

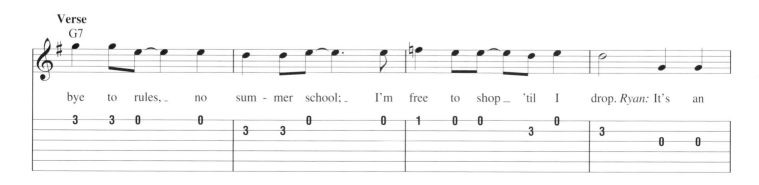

Verse

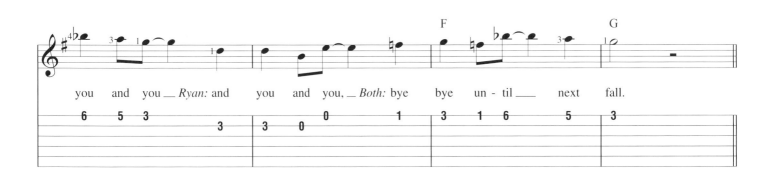

Pre-Chorus

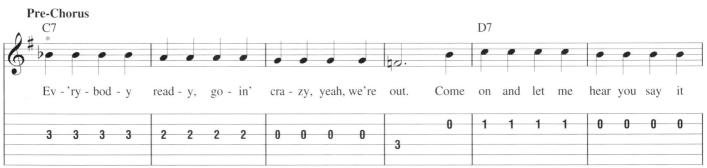

*Sung one octave higher, next 7½ meas.

Chorus

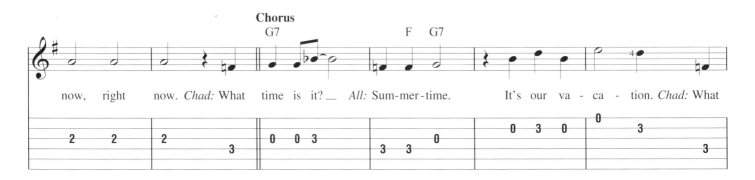

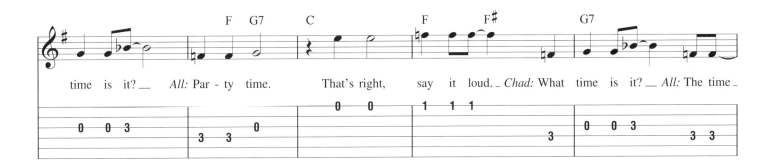

time is it? _ *All:* Par - ty time. That's right, say it loud. _ *Chad:* What time is it? _ *All:* The time _

_ of our lives. An - ti - ci - pa - tion. *Chad:* What time is it? _ *All:* Sum - mer - time. School's out.

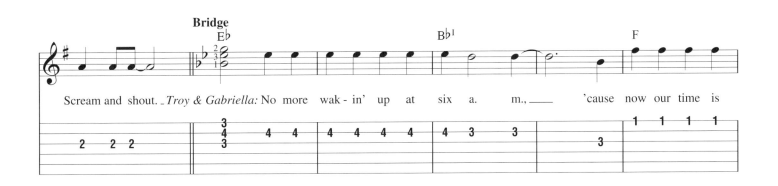

Bridge

Scream and shout. _ *Troy & Gabriella:* No more wak - in' up at six a. m., _ 'cause now our time is

all our own. _____ *Sharpay & Ryan:* E - nough al - read - y, we're wait - ing, come on, _ let's

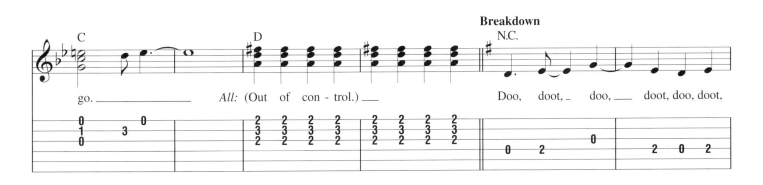

Breakdown

go. _____ *All:* (Out of con - trol.) _ Doo, doot, _ doo, _ doot, doo, doot,

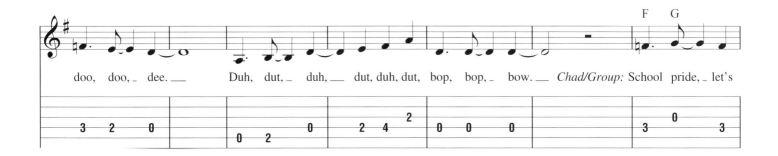

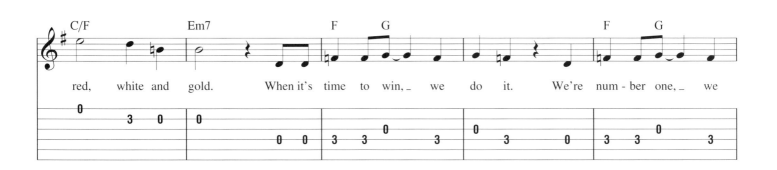

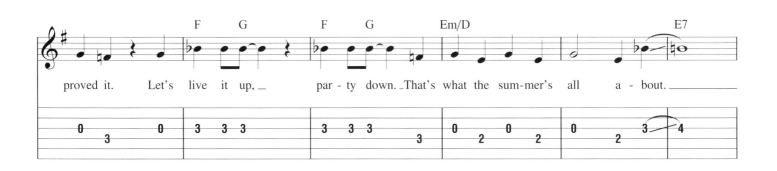

Outro

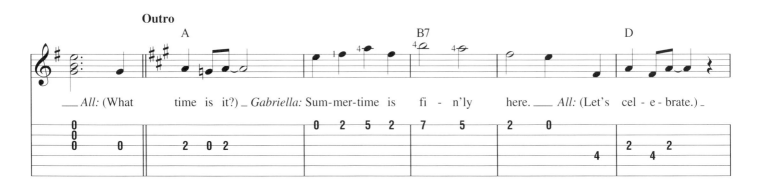

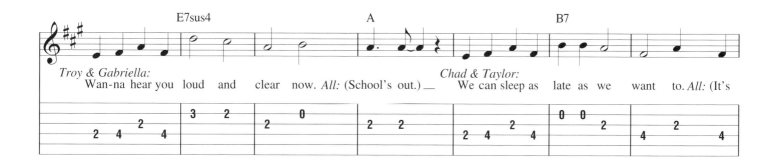

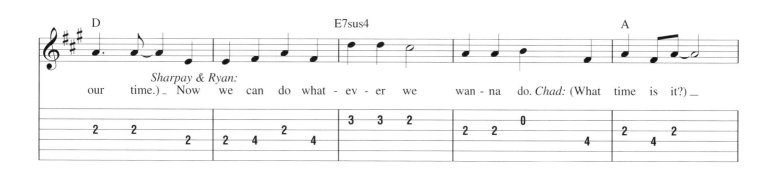

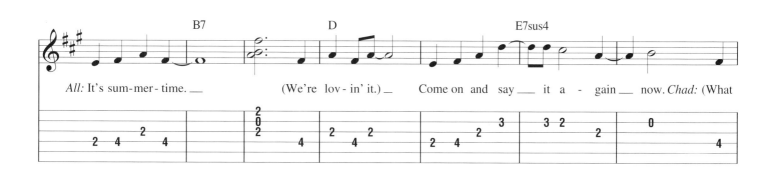

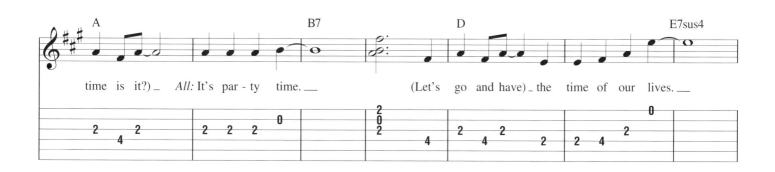

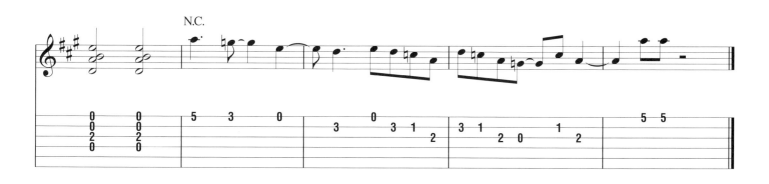

Fabulous

Words and Music by David Lawrence and Faye Greenberg

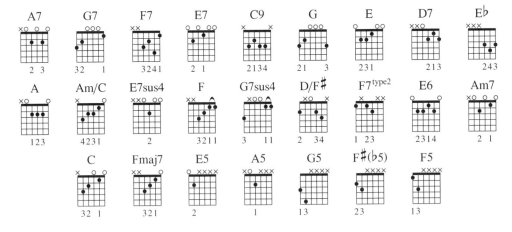

*Capo III

Strum Pattern: 3, 4
Pick Pattern: 3, 4

Intro
Freely

Sharpay: It's out with the old ___ and in with the new. ___ Good - bye, clouds of gray; hel -

*Optional: To match recording, place capo at 3rd fret.

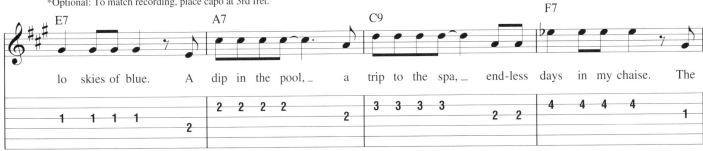

lo skies of blue. A dip in the pool, ___ a trip to the spa, ___ end-less days in my chaise. The

Verse
Moderately

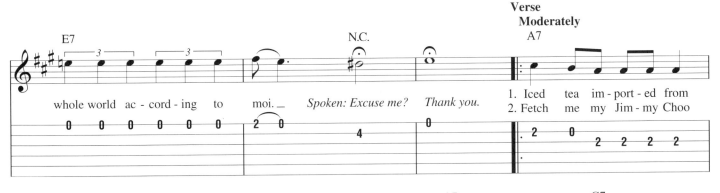

whole world ac - cord - ing to moi. *Spoken: Excuse me? Thank you.*

1. Iced tea im - port - ed from
2. Fetch me my Jim - my Choo

Eng - land, life-guards im - port - ed from Spain, tow - els im - port - ed from Tur - key, and
flip - flops. Where is my pink Pra - da tote? I need my Tif - fa - ny hair - band, and

© 2007 Walt Disney Music Company
All Rights Reserved Used by Permission

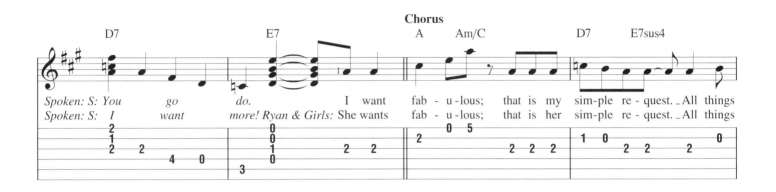

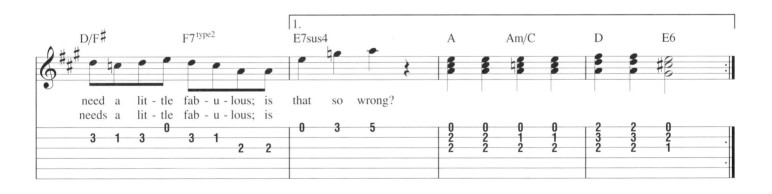

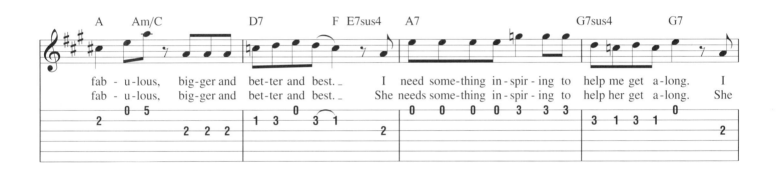

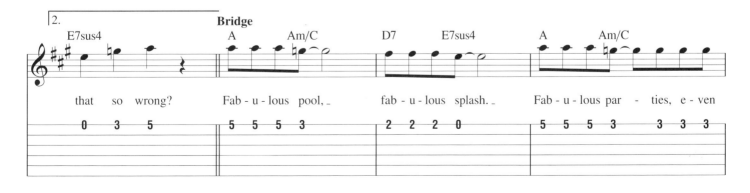

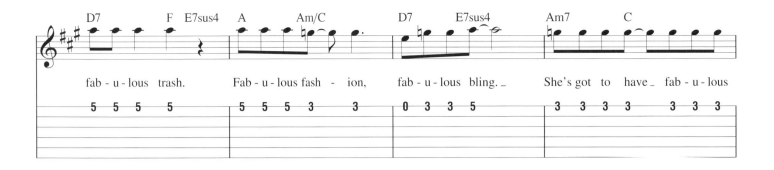

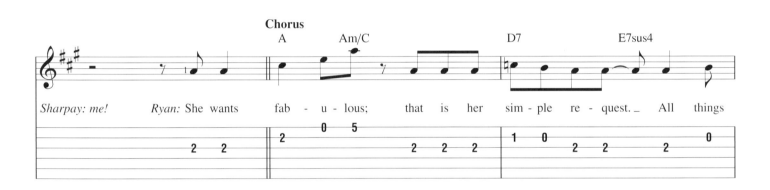

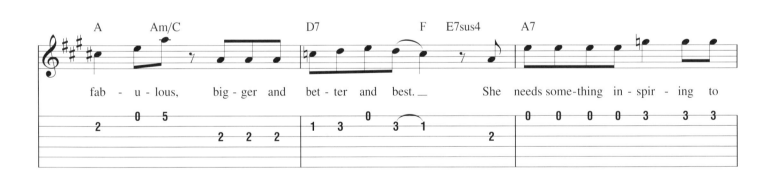

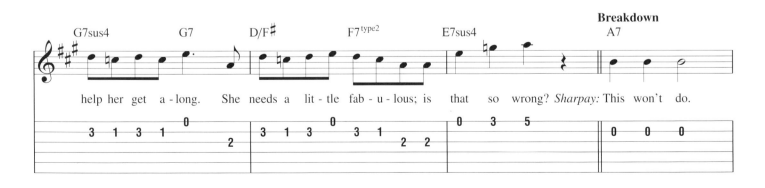

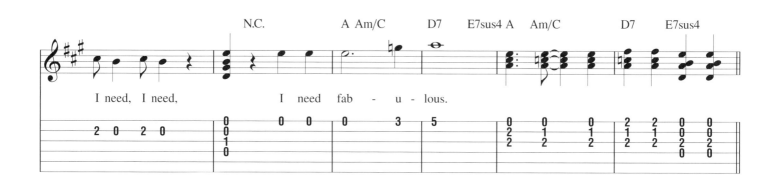

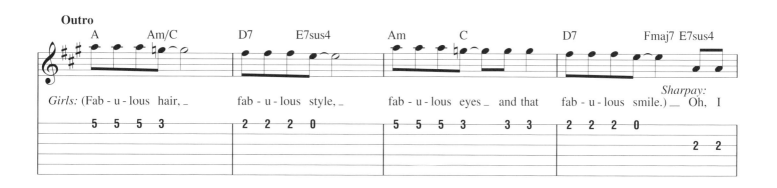

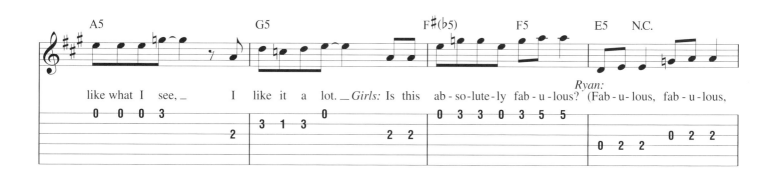

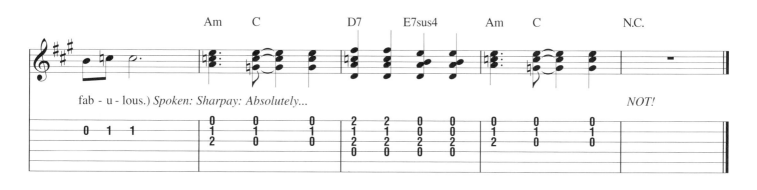

Work This Out

Words and Music by Randy Petersen and Kevin Quinn

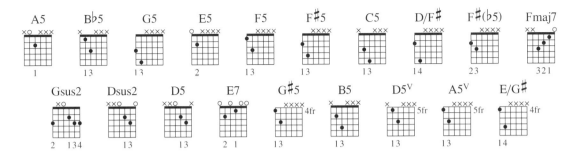

*Capo I

Verse
Moderately fast

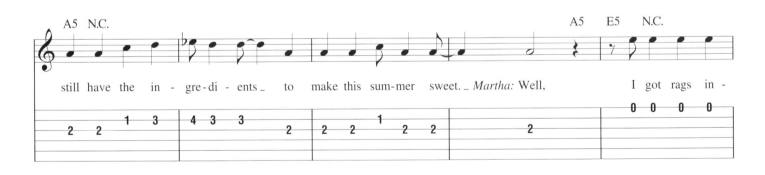

1. *Chad:* How did we get from the top of the world to the bot-tom of the heap?

*Optional: To match recording, place capo at 1st fret.

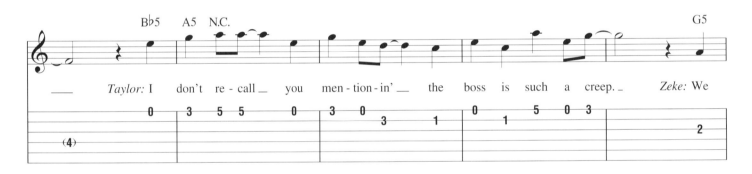

Taylor: I don't re-call you men-tion-in' the boss is such a creep. *Zeke:* We

still have the in-gre-di-ents to make this sum-mer sweet. *Martha:* Well, I got rags in-

stead of rich - es, *Jason:* and all these dirt-y dish - es. *All:* Just wish I had three wish -

%: **Chorus**

- es. _____ _Gabriella: Okay, guys, break it up._ _Troy:_ We've got to work, work, to

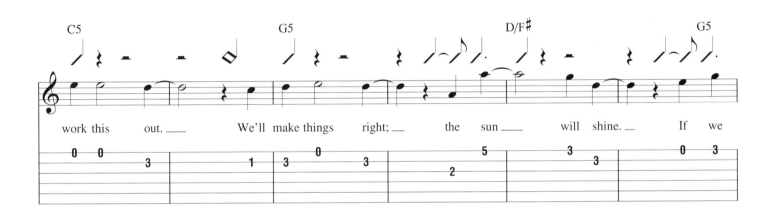

work this out. ___ We'll make things right; ___ the sun ___ will shine. ___ If we

To Coda ⊕

work, work, there'll be no doubt. ___ We can still save the

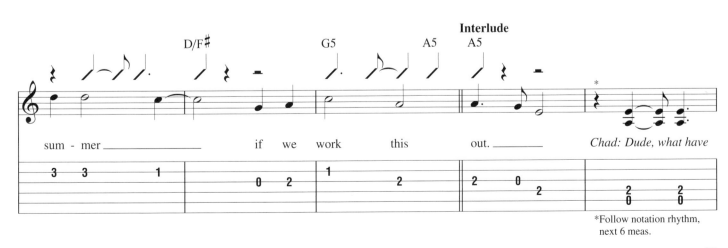

Interlude

sum - mer _____ if we work this out. _____ _Chad: Dude, what have_

*Follow notation rhythm,
next 6 meas.

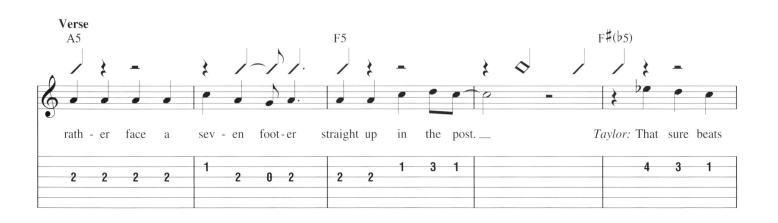

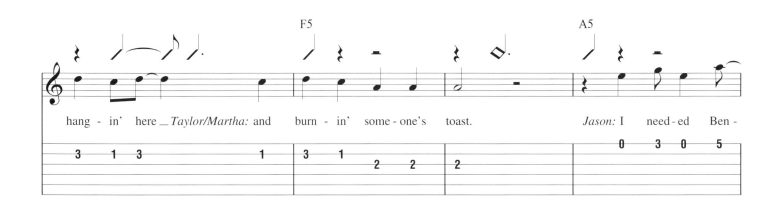

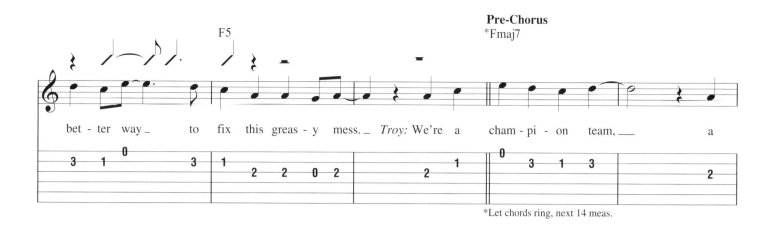

*Let chords ring, next 14 meas.

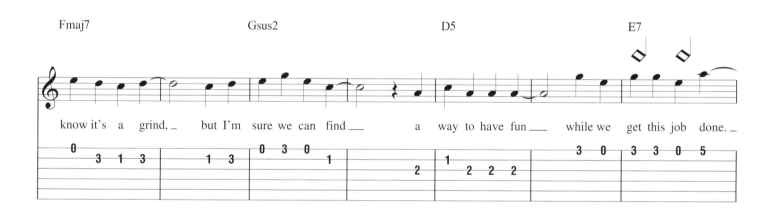

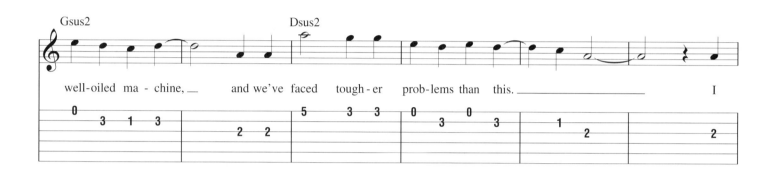

17

Interlude
A5

Bridge
A5

out. _____

Troy: Let's work it.   Tell   me   what   you   want. __

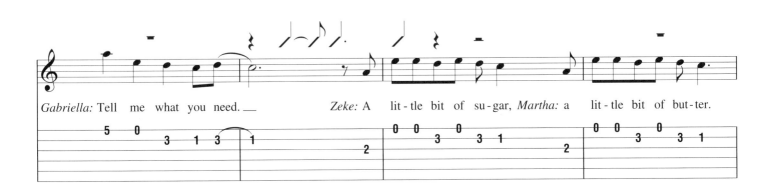

Gabriella: Tell   me   what   you   need. __   *Zeke:* A   lit - tle   bit   of   su - gar, *Martha:* a   lit - tle   bit   of   but - ter.

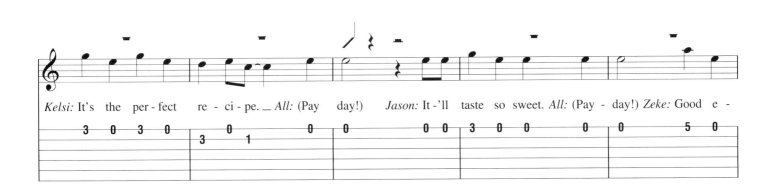

Kelsi: It's   the   per - fect   re - ci - pe. __ *All:* (Pay   day!)   *Jason:* It -'ll   taste   so   sweet. *All:* (Pay - day!) *Zeke:* Good   e -

E5

E5   F5   N.C.

nough   to   eat.   *Jason:* Gon - na   make   some   mo - tion   pic - tures.   *Martha:* Hit   the   mall   with

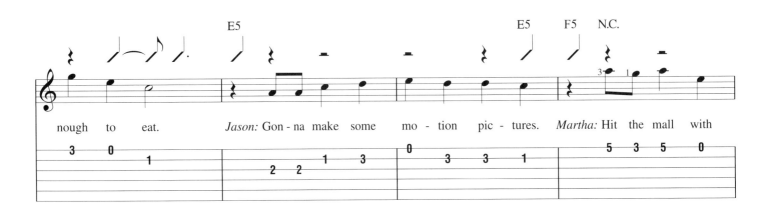

18

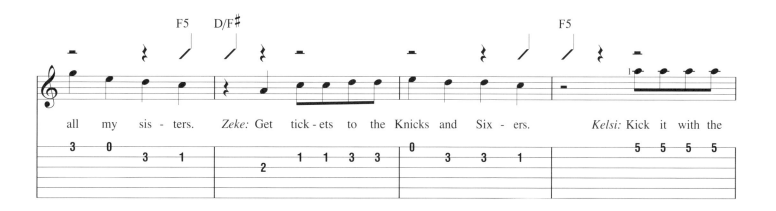

all my sis - ters. *Zeke:* Get tick - ets to the Knicks and Six - ers. *Kelsi:* Kick it with the

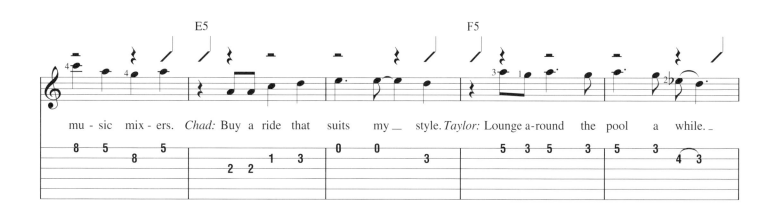

mu - sic mix - ers. *Chad:* Buy a ride that suits my __ style. *Taylor:* Lounge a-round the pool a while. __

Troy: Make a date with my fav - 'rite girl. *Troy/Gabriella:* We've got it made. _____ *All:* Whoa, _____

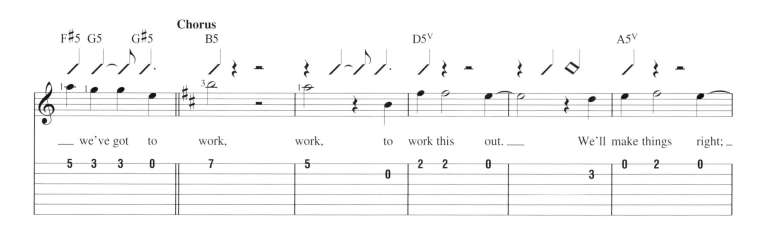

__ we've got to work, work, to work this out. __ We'll make things right; __

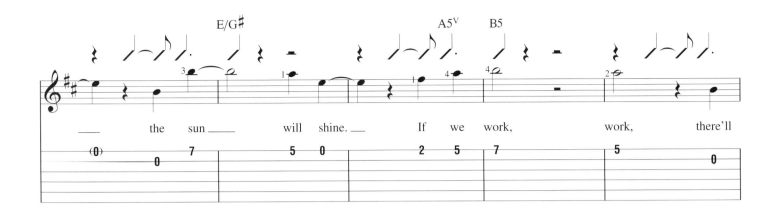

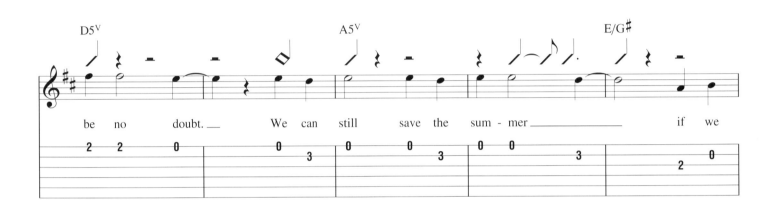

I Don't Dance

Words and Music by Matthew Gerrard and Robbie Nevil

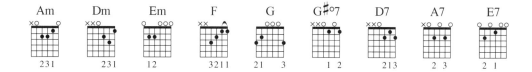

Strum Pattern: 4
Pick Pattern: 1

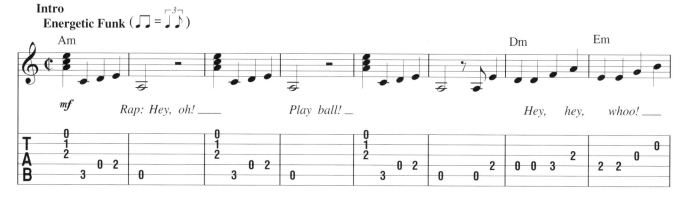

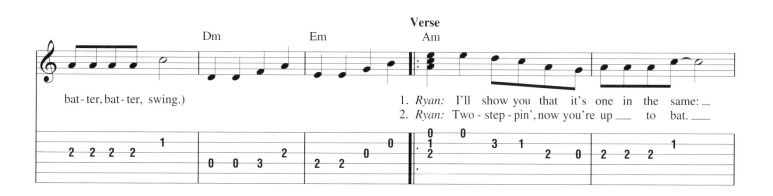

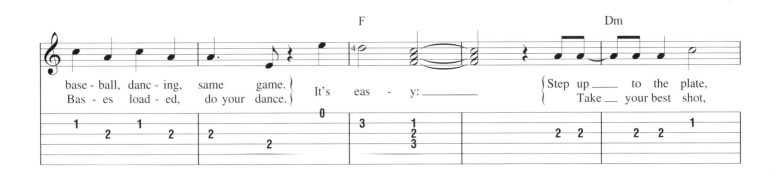

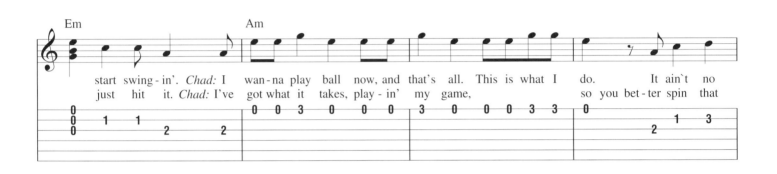

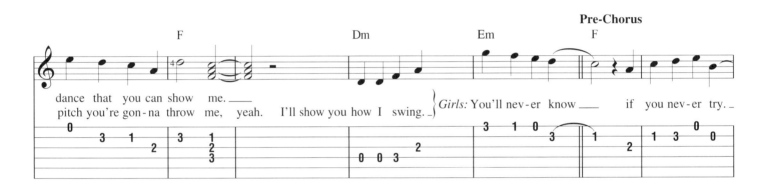

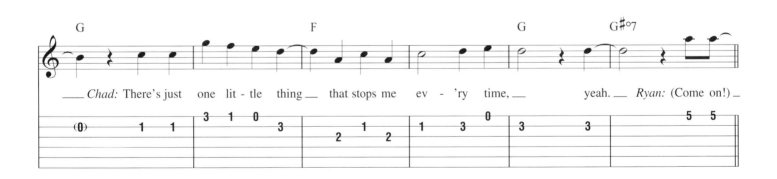

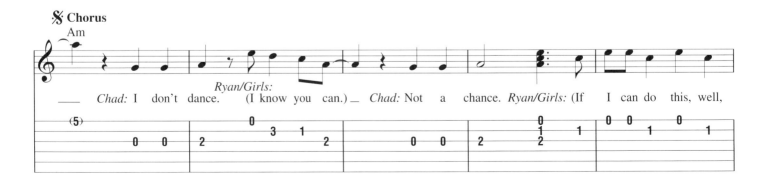

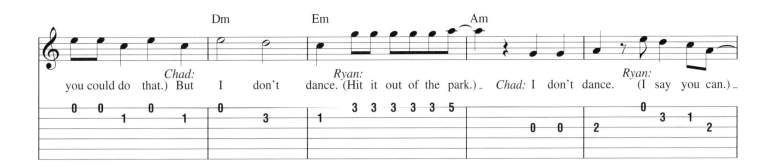

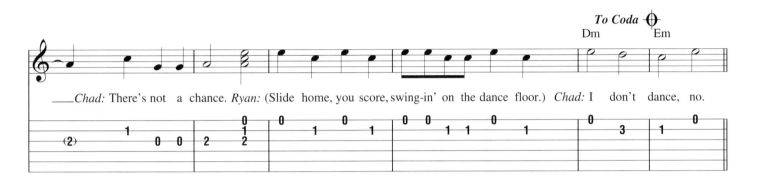

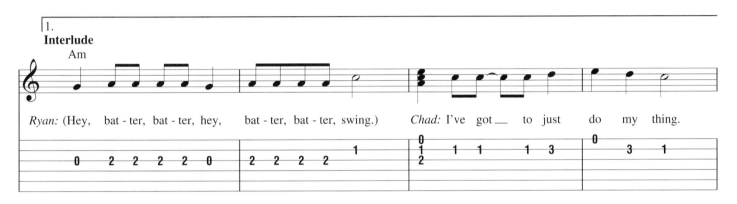

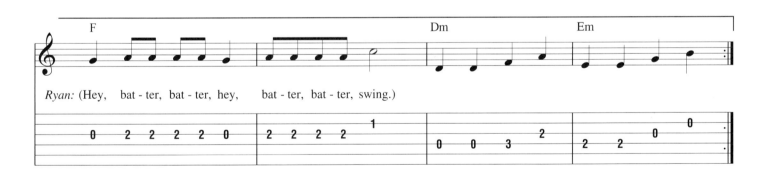

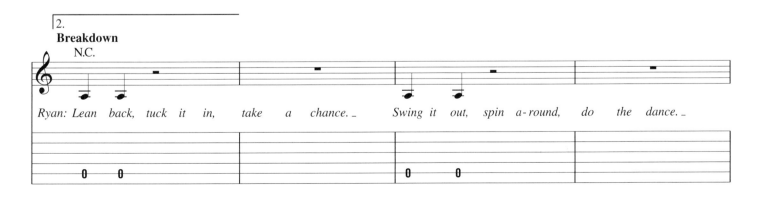

Chad: I wan-na play ball, not dance hall. I'm mak-in' a tri-ple, not a cur-tain call.

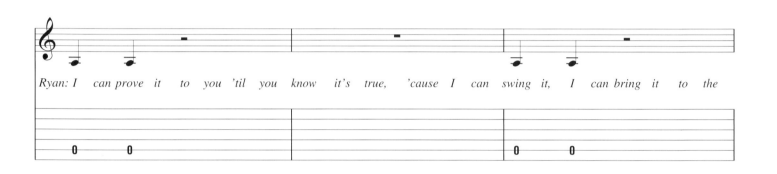

Ryan: I can prove it to you 'til you know it's true, 'cause I can swing it, I can bring it to the

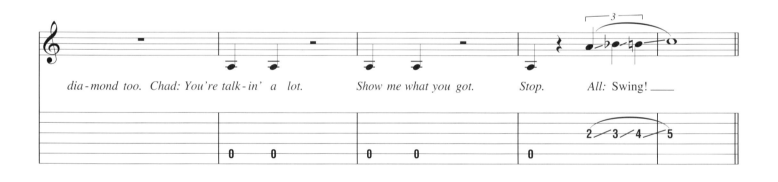

dia-mond too. Chad: You're talk-in' a lot. Show me what you got. Stop. All: Swing! ____

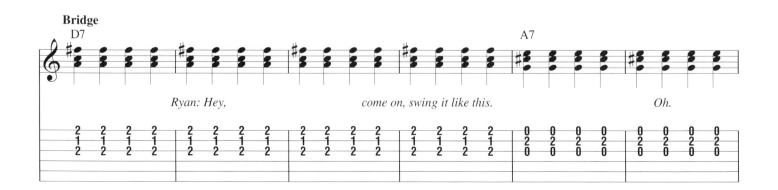

Bridge

Ryan: Hey, come on, swing it like this. Oh.

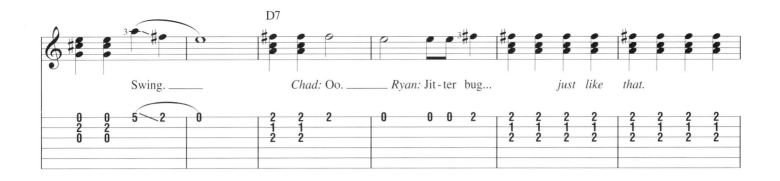

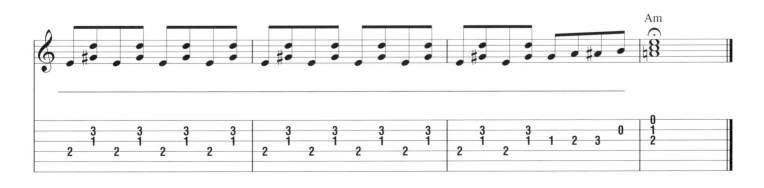

You Are the Music in Me

Words and Music by Jamie Houston

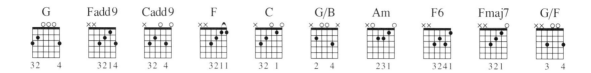

*Capo V

Strum Pattern: 4, 6
Pick Pattern: 4, 5

Intro
Moderately

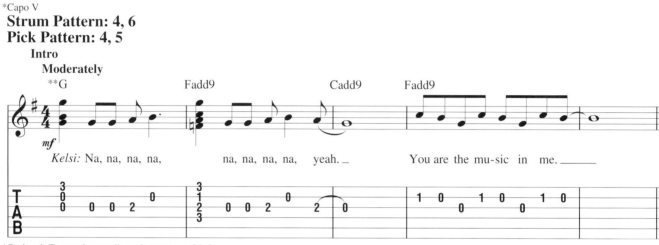

Kelsi: Na, na, na, na, na, na, na, na, yeah. ___ You are the mu-sic in me. ___

*Optional: To match recording, place capo at 5th fret.

**Let chords ring next 4 meas.

Verse

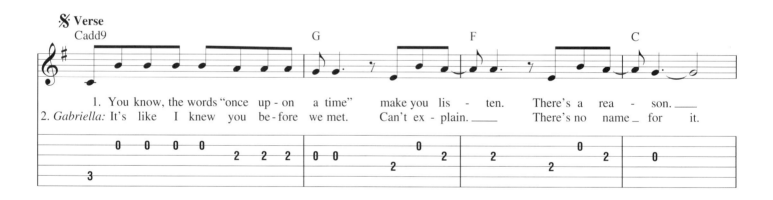

1. You know, the words "once up-on a time" make you lis-ten. There's a rea-son. ___
2. Gabriella: It's like I knew you be-fore we met. Can't ex-plain. ___ There's no name_ for it.

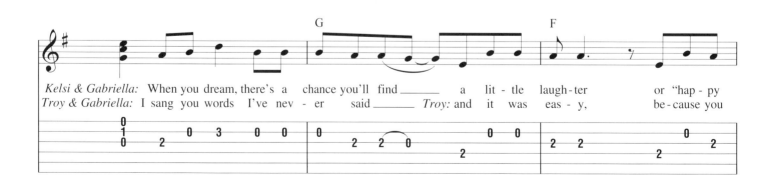

Kelsi & Gabriella: When you dream, there's a chance you'll find ___ a lit-tle laugh-ter or "hap-py
Troy & Gabriella: I sang you words I've nev-er said ___ Troy: and it was eas-y, be-cause you

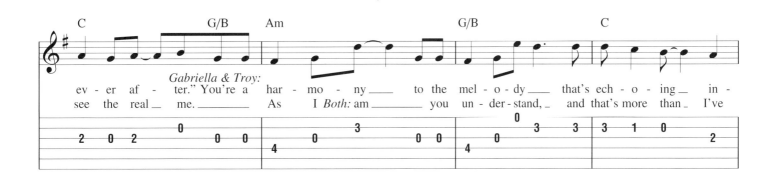

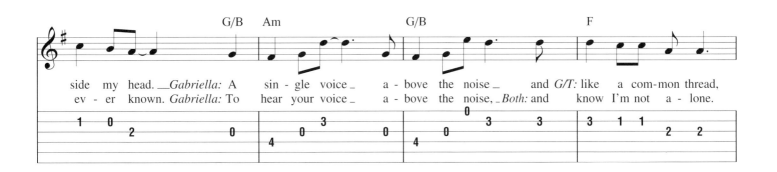

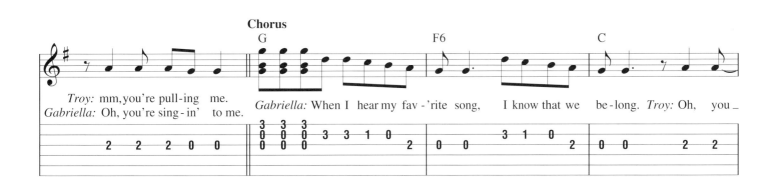

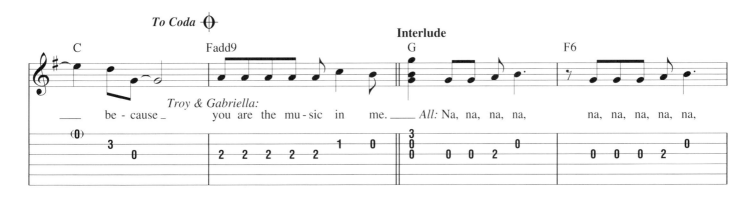

D.S. al Coda

⊕ **Coda**

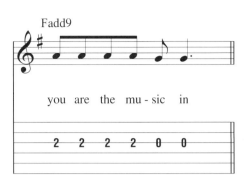

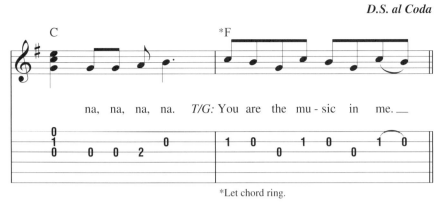

*Let chord ring.

Bridge

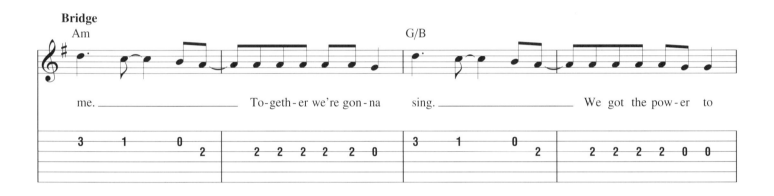

Interlude

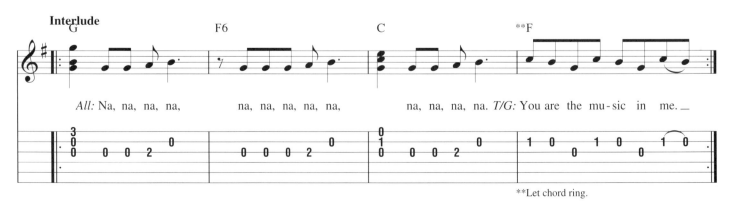

**Let chord ring.

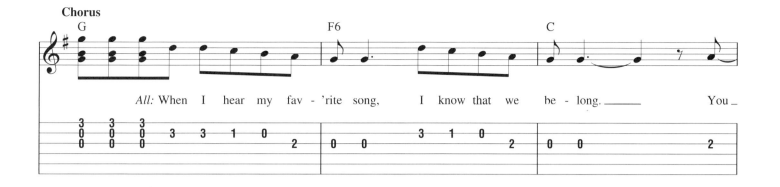

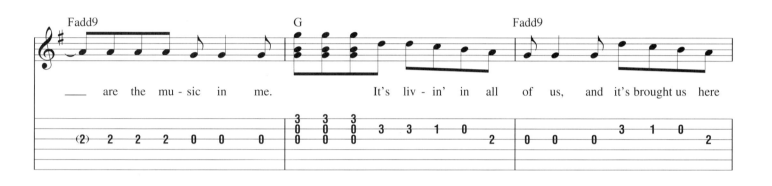

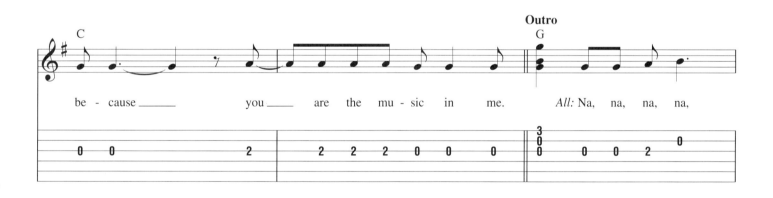

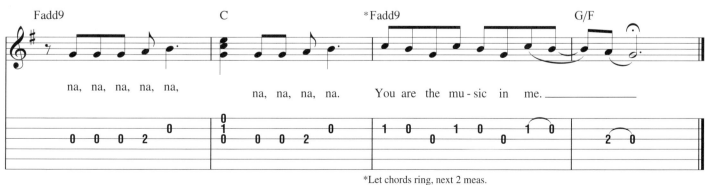

*Let chords ring, next 2 meas.

Gotta Go My Own Way

Words and Music by Adam Watts and Andy Dodd

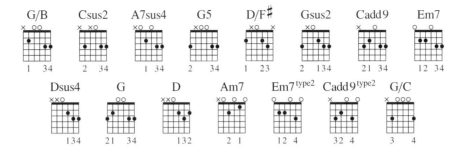

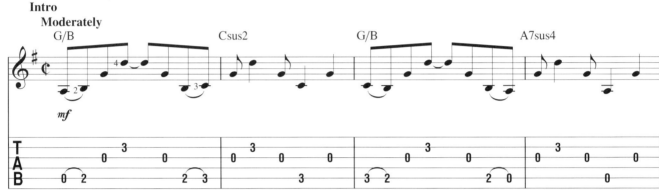

*Capo II

Strum Pattern: 4
Pick Pattern: 1, 6

Intro
Moderately

*Optional: To match recording, place capo at 2nd fret.

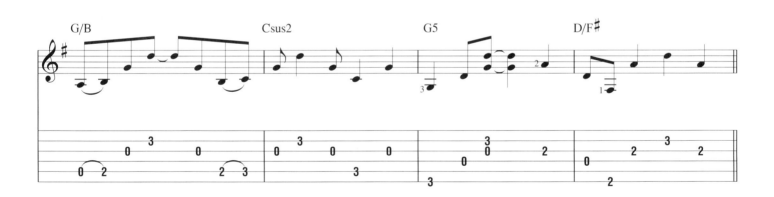

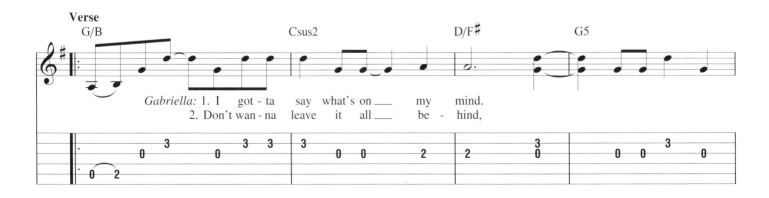

Gabriella: 1. I got-ta say what's on ___ my mind.
2. Don't wan-na leave it all ___ be-hind,

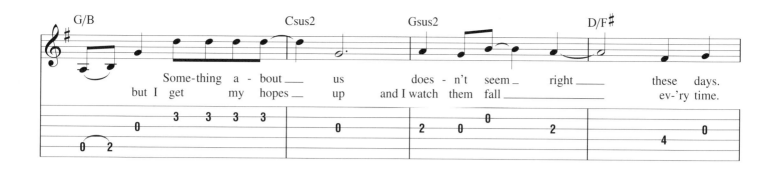

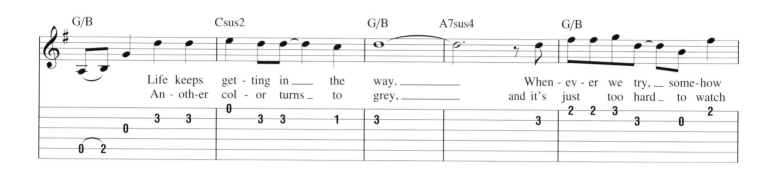

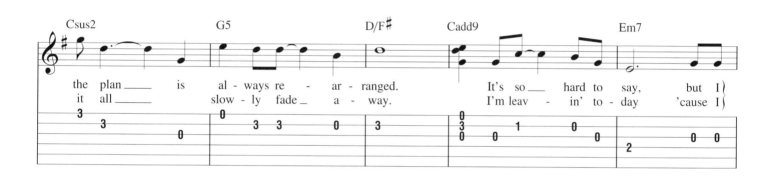

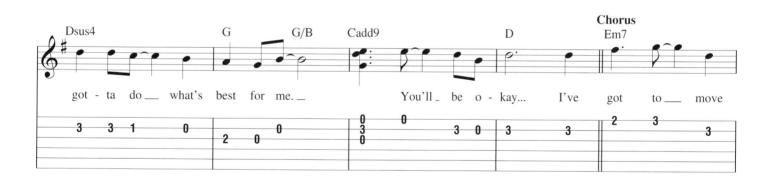

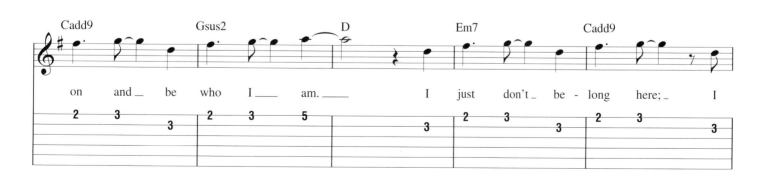

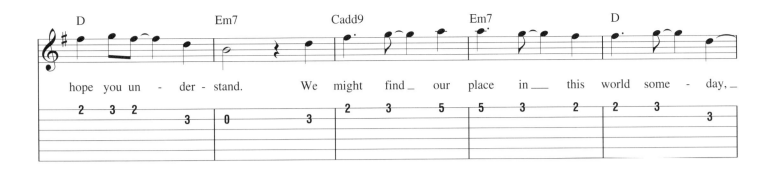

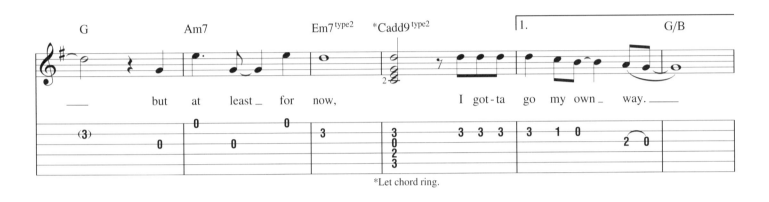

*Let chord ring.

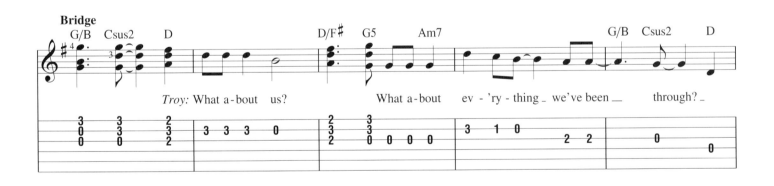

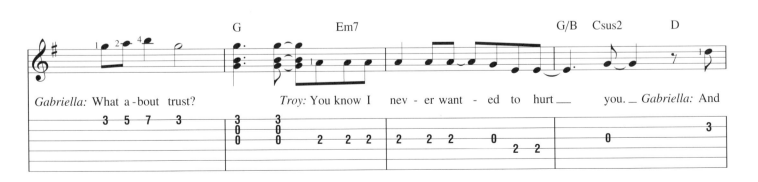

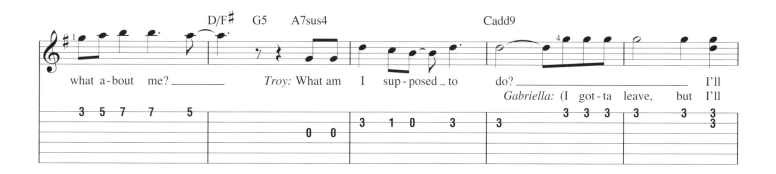

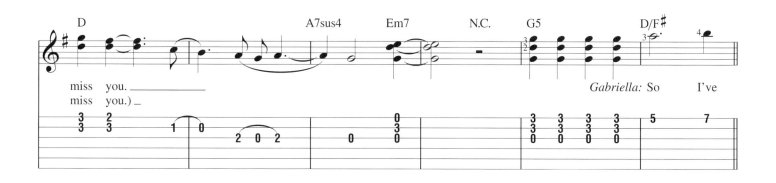

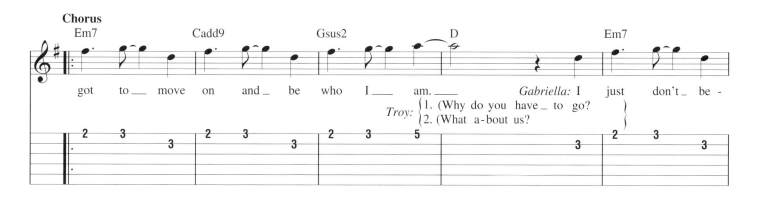

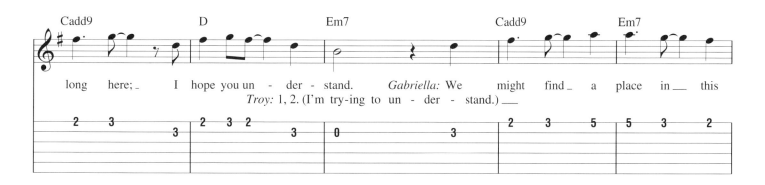

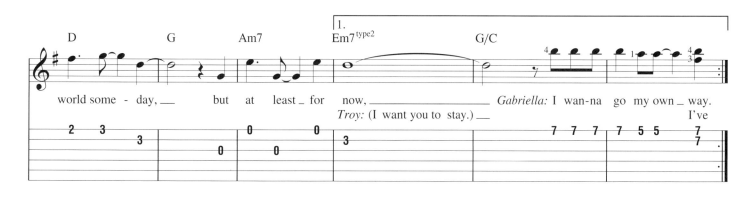

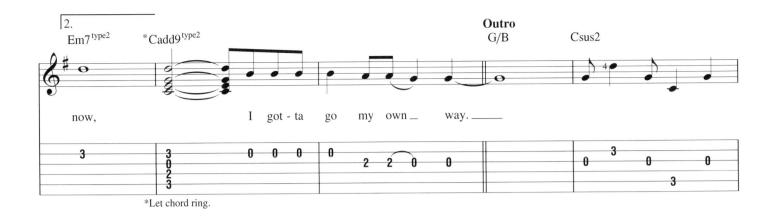

now,　　　　I got-ta go my own ___ way. ___

*Let chord ring.

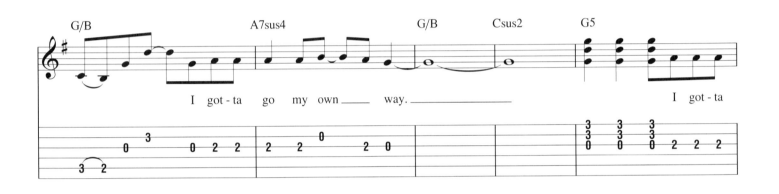

I got-ta go my own ___ way. ___　　　　　I got-ta

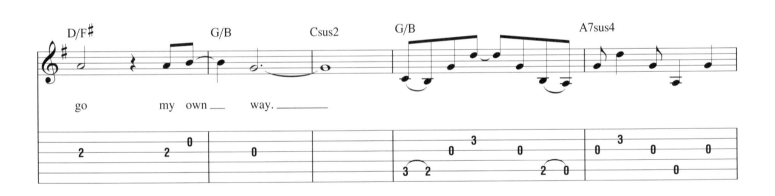

go　　　my own ___ way.

Everyday

Words and Music by Jamie Houston

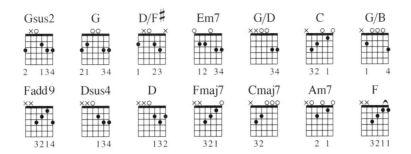

Strum Pattern: 4
Pick Pattern: 5

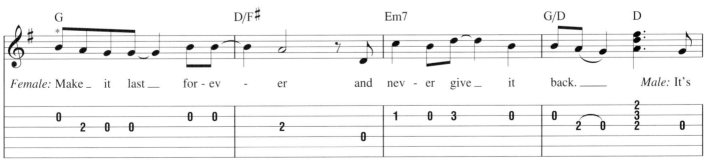

*Sung one octave higher throughout.

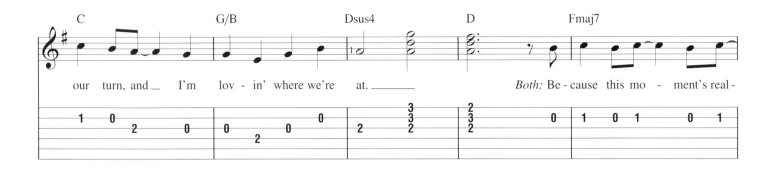

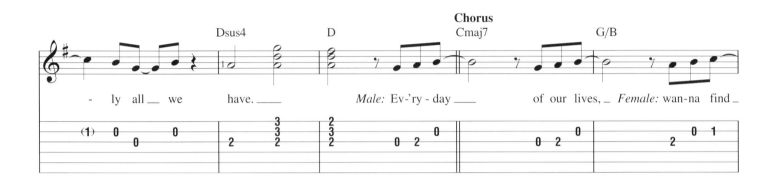

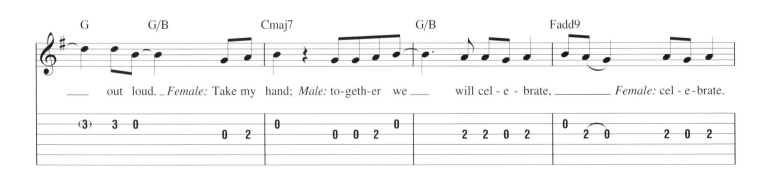

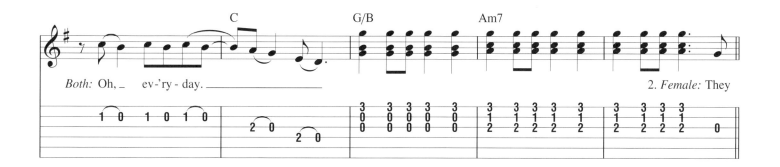

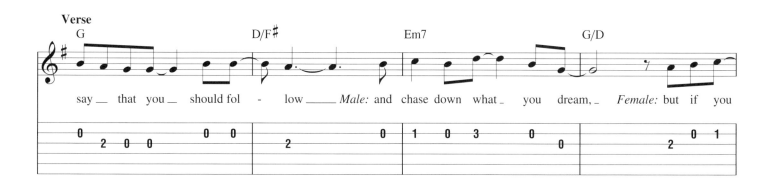

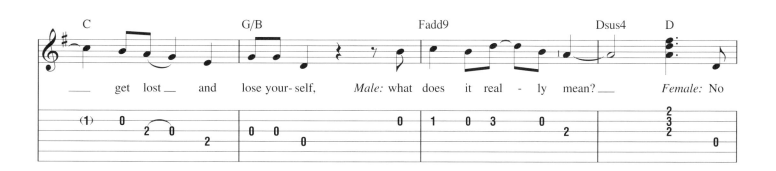

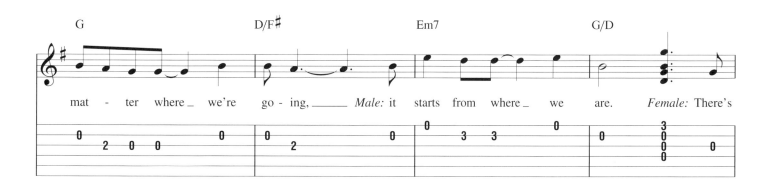

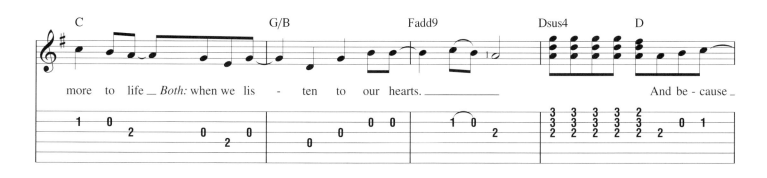

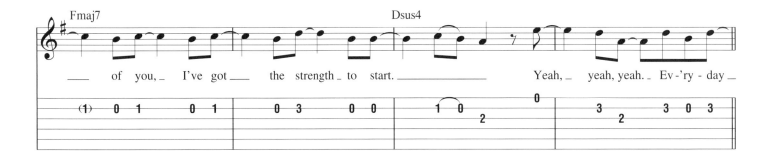

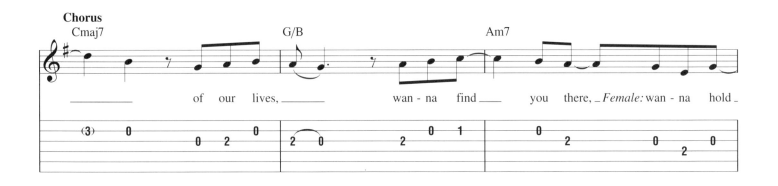

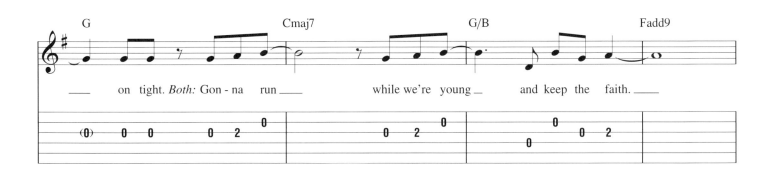

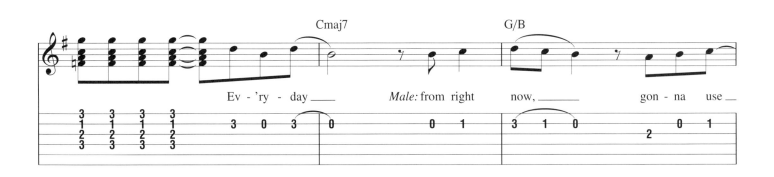

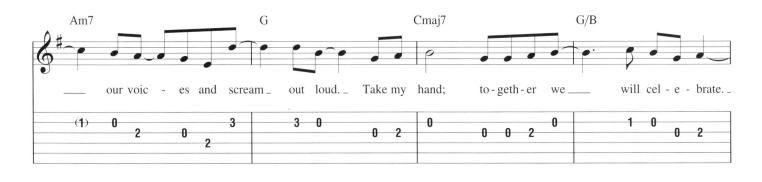

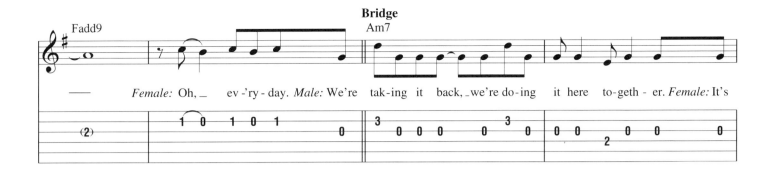

Bridge

—— *Female:* Oh, — ev -'ry - day. *Male:* We're tak-ing it back, —we're do-ing it here to-geth - er. *Female:* It's

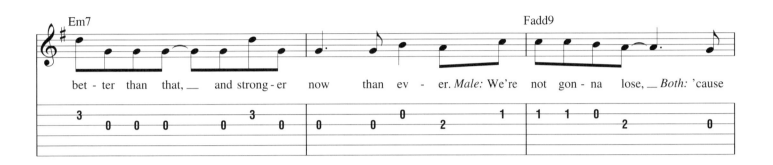

bet - ter than that, — and strong - er now than ev - er. *Male:* We're not gon - na lose, — *Both:* 'cause

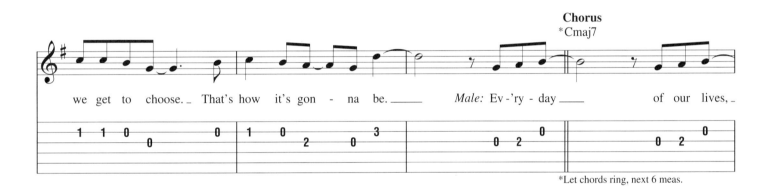

Chorus

we get to choose. — That's how it's gon - na be. ——— *Male:* Ev -'ry - day —— of our lives, —

*Let chords ring, next 6 meas.

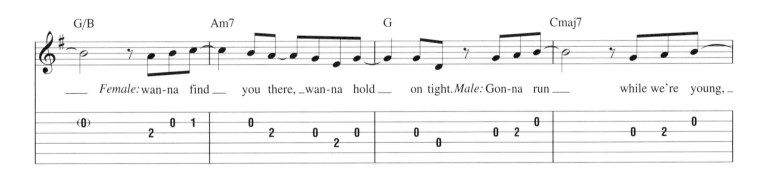

—— *Female:* wan-na find — you there, —wan-na hold — on tight. *Male:* Gon-na run — while we're young, —

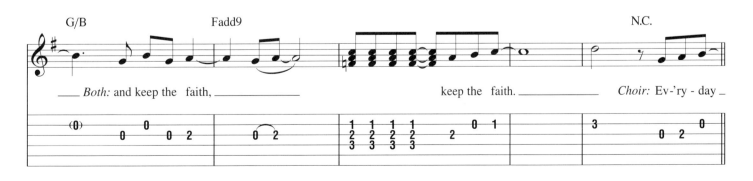

—— *Both:* and keep the faith, ——————— keep the faith. —————— *Choir:* Ev-'ry - day —

39

Chorus

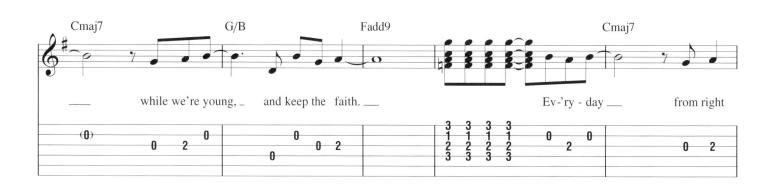

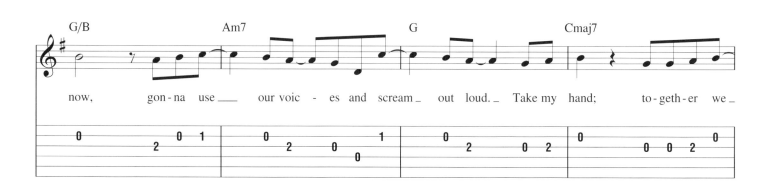

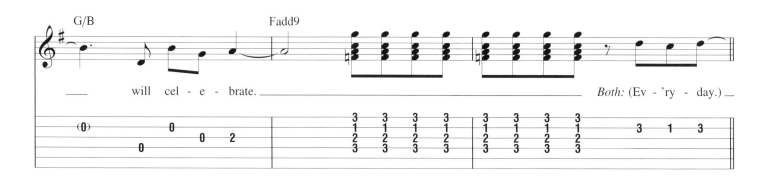

Breakdown

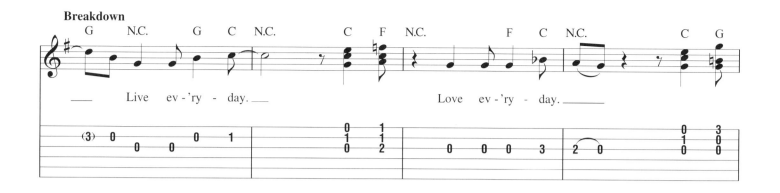

Live ev-'ry - day. _____   Love ev-'ry - day. _____

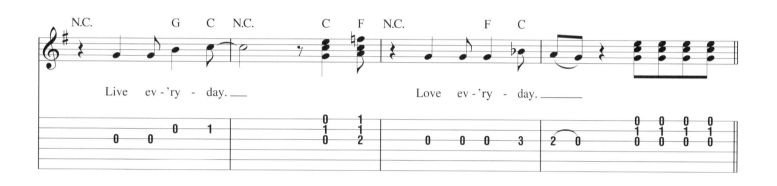

Live ev-'ry - day. _____   Love ev-'ry - day. _____

Outro

Ev-'ry - day, ___   ev-'ry - day, ___   ev-'ry - day, ___   ev-'ry - day. __

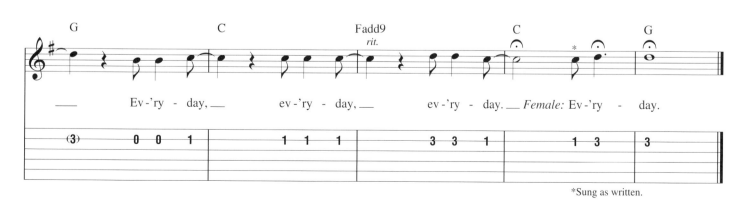

_____ Ev-'ry - day, ___   ev-'ry - day, ___   ev-'ry - day. ___ *Female:* Ev-'ry - day.

*Sung as written.

Bet on It

Words and Music by Tim James and Antonina Armato

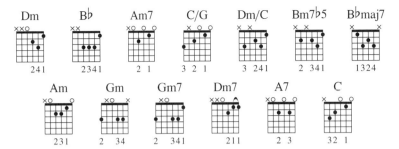

*Tune down 1 step:
(low to high) D-G-C-F-A-D

Strum Pattern: 3, 4
Pick Pattern: 2, 5

Verse
Modertately

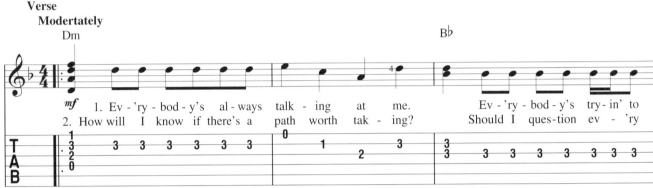

1. Ev - 'ry - bod - y's al - ways talk - ing at me. Ev - 'ry - bod - y's try - in' to
2. How will I know if there's a path worth tak - ing? Should I ques - tion ev - 'ry

*Optional: To match recording, tune down 1 step.

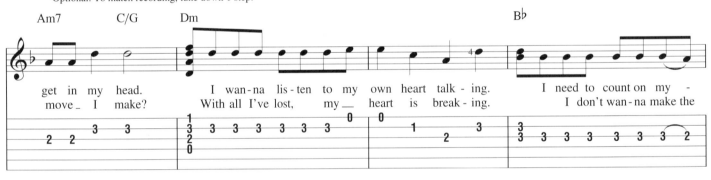

get in my head. I wan - na lis - ten to my own heart talk - ing. I need to count on my -
move _ I make? With all I've lost, my _ heart is break - ing. I don't wan - na make the

self in - stead.} (Did you ev - er) {lose _ your - self to {get what you want? } (Did you ev - er) {get on a ride, then
same mis - takes. {doubt _ your dream will {ev - er come true?} {blame _ the world but

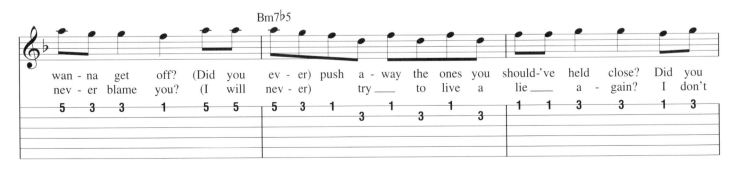

wan - na get off? (Did you ev - er) push a - way the ones you should - 've held close? Did you
nev - er blame you? (I will nev - er) try ___ to live a lie ___ a - gain? I don't

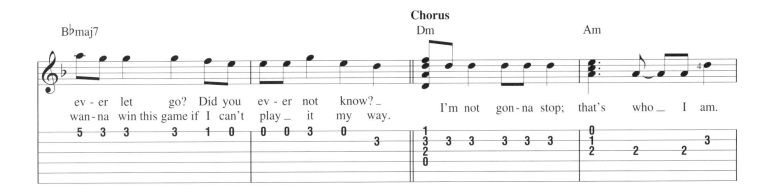

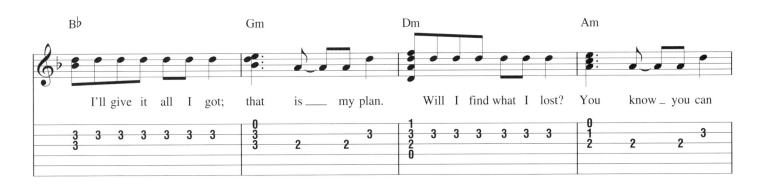

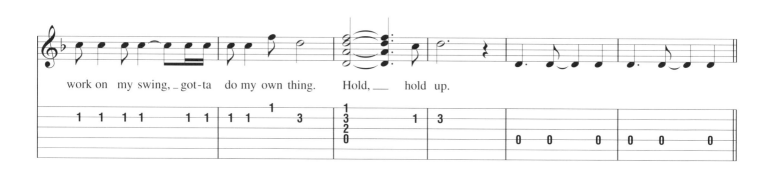

Bridge

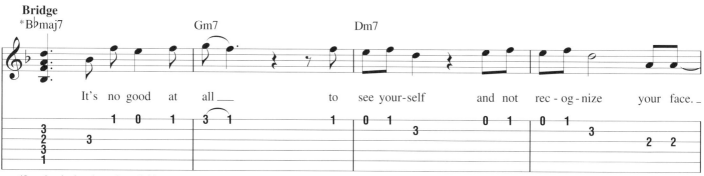

*Let chords ring throughout Bridge.

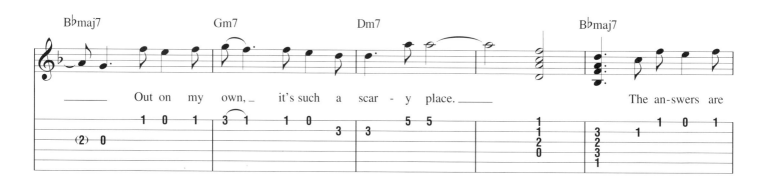

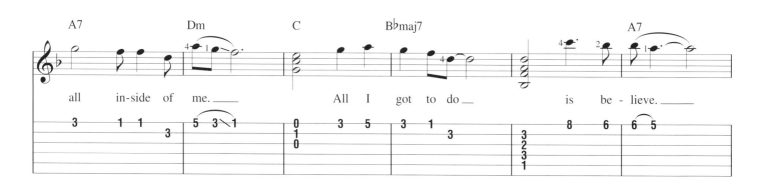

Outro-Chorus

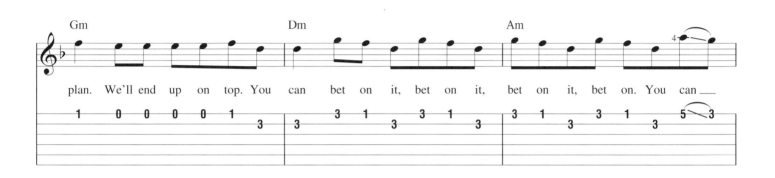

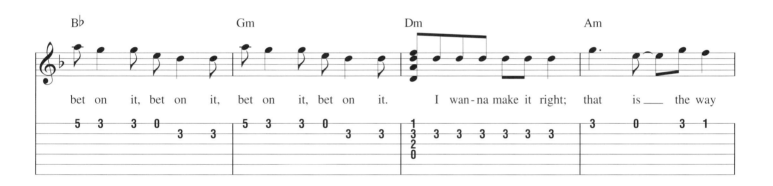

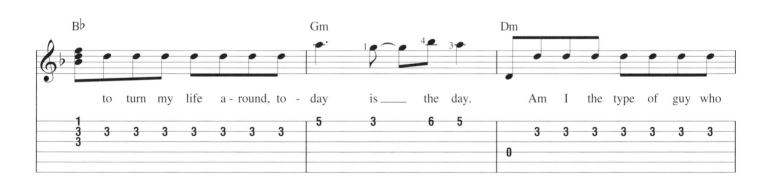

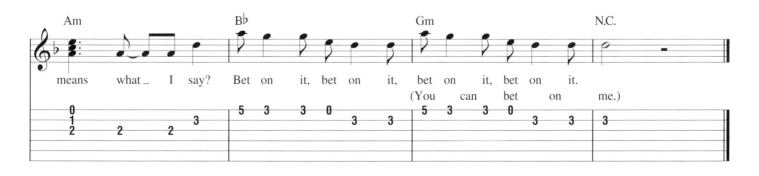

All for One

Words and Music by Matthew Gerrard and Robbie Nevil

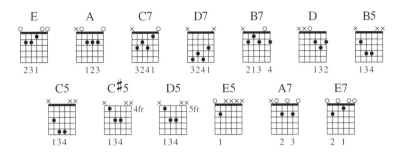

Strum Pattern: 3, 4
Pick Pattern: 1, 6

Verse
Moderately fast

1. *Troy:* The sum-mer that we want-ed, *Ryan:* yeah, we fi-n'lly got it. *Chad:* Now's the time we get to share. _

_ *Sharpay:* Each day we'll be to-geth-er *Taylor:* now un-til for-ev-er, *Gabriella:* so ev-'ry-bod-y ev-'ry-where,

Pre-Chorus

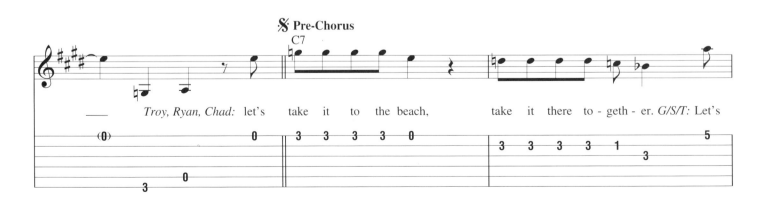

_ *Troy, Ryan, Chad:* let's take it to the beach, take it there to-geth-er. *G/S/T:* Let's

Chorus

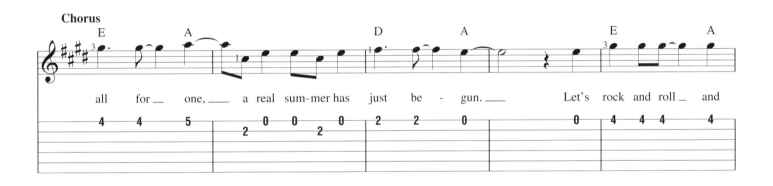

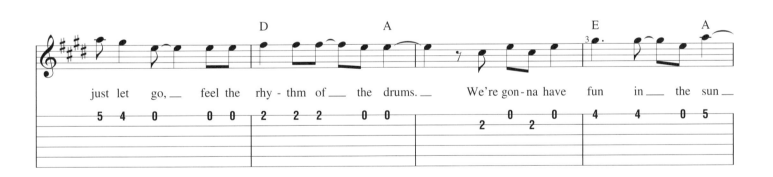

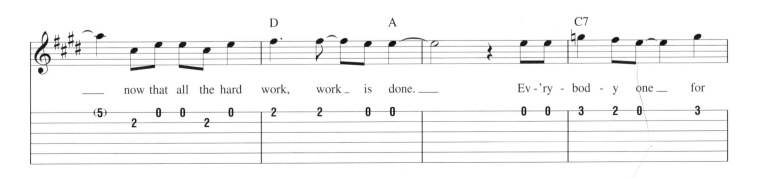

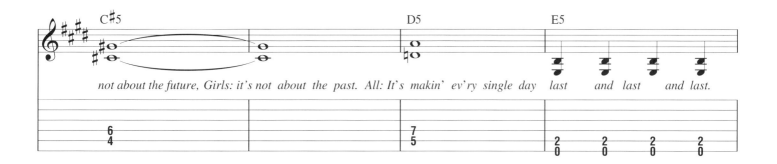

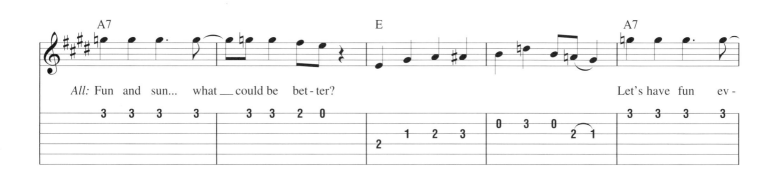

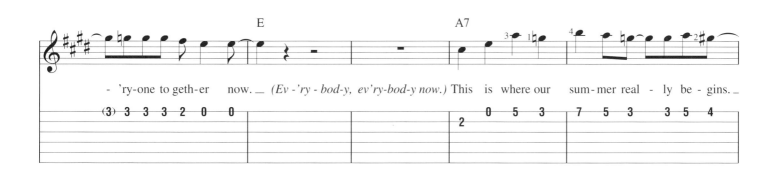

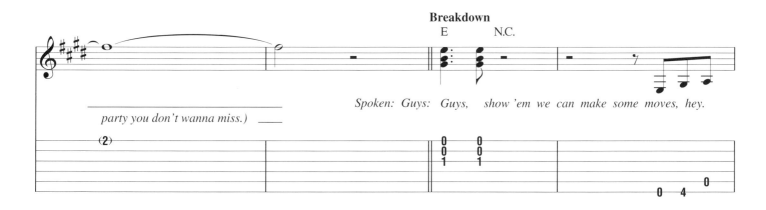

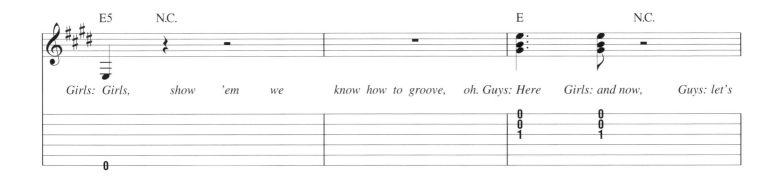

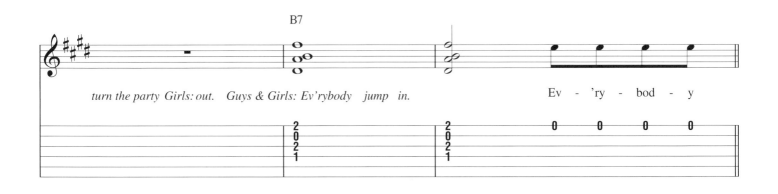

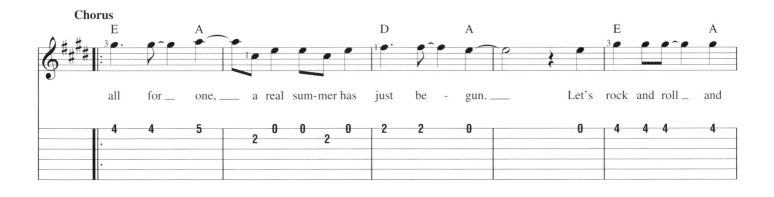

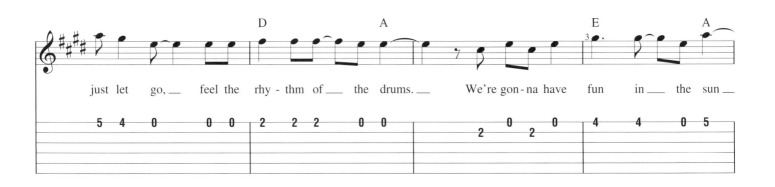

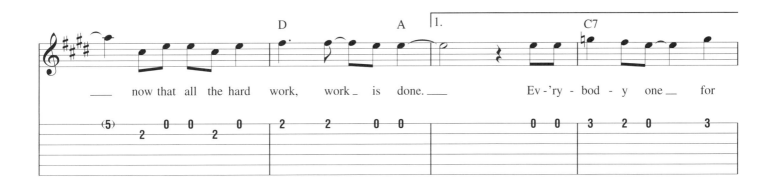

____ now that all the hard work, work_ is done. ___ Ev -'ry - bod - y one __ for_

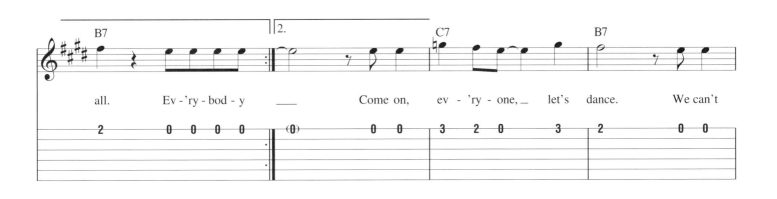

_all. Ev -'ry - bod - y ___ Come on, ev -'ry - one,_ let's dance. We can't_

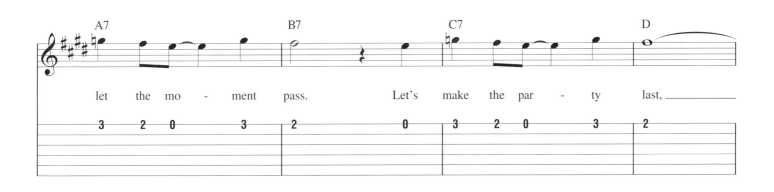

_let the mo - ment pass. Let's make the par - ty last, _____

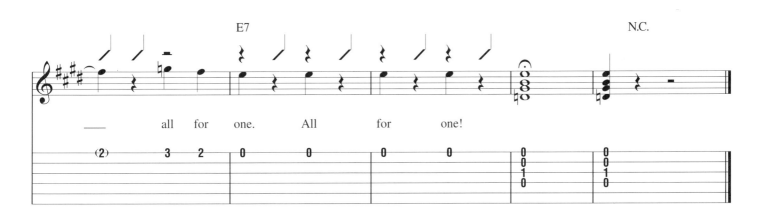

____ all for one. All for one!_

Humu Humu Nuku Nuku Apuaa

Words and Music by David Lawrence and Faye Greenberg

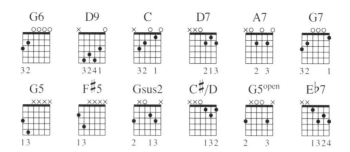

*Capo II

Strum Pattern: 2, 4

Pick Pattern: 3, 6

Intro

Moderately fast

1. *Ryan:* A

*Optional: To match recording, place capo at 2nd fret.

Verse

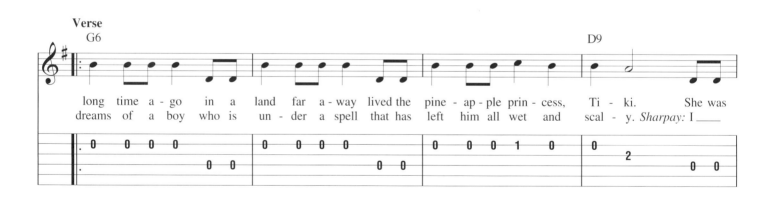

long time a - go in a land far a - way lived the pine - ap - ple prin - cess, Ti - ki. She was

dreams of a boy who is un - der a spell that has left him all wet and scal - y. *Sharpay:* I

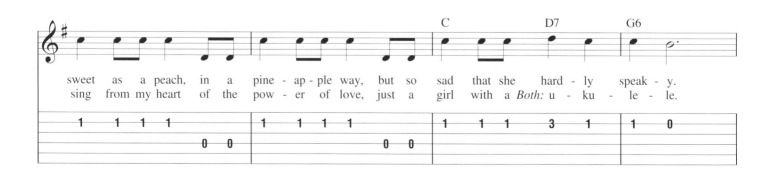

sweet as a peach, in a pine - ap - ple way, but so sad that she hard - ly speak - y.

sing from my heart of the pow - er of love, just a girl with a *Both:* u - ku - le - le.

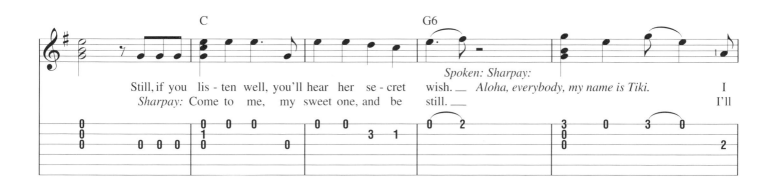

Still, if you lis-ten well, you'll hear her se-cret wish. __ *Spoken: Sharpay:* *Aloha, everybody, my name is Tiki.* I
Sharpay: Come to me, my sweet one, and be still. __ I'll

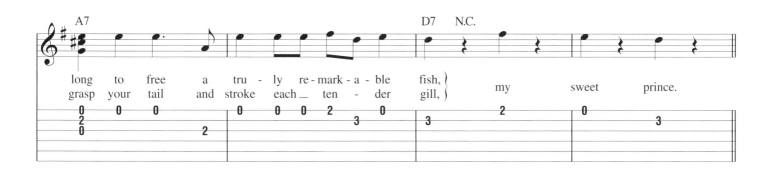

long to free a tru-ly re-mark-a-ble fish, } my sweet prince.
grasp your tail and stroke each __ ten-der gill, }

𝄋 **Chorus**

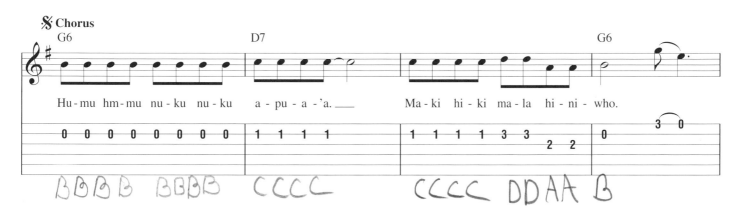

Hu-mu hm-mu nu-ku nu-ku a-pu-a-'a. __ Ma-ki hi-ki ma-la hi-ni who.

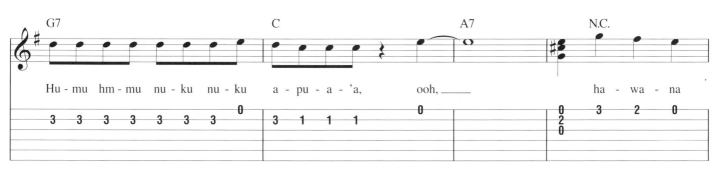

Hu-mu hm-mu nu-ku nu-ku a-pu-a-'a, ooh, ____ ha-wa-na

To Coda ⊕ |1.

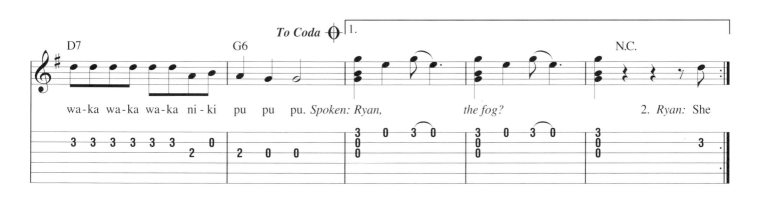

wa-ka wa-ka wa-ka ni-ki pu pu pu. *Spoken: Ryan,* *the fog?* 2. *Ryan:* She

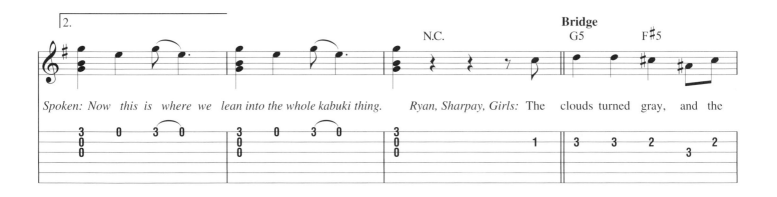

Spoken: Now this is where we lean into the whole kabuki thing. *Ryan, Sharpay, Girls:* The clouds turned gray, and the

big sky cried, and the o - cean had a fit. *Spoken: Sharpay: Ryan! Where's my ocean?!* *S/R/G:* Then the

wind went whoosh, and thun - der cracked, and might - y Mount Fu - fu spit. *Sharpay:* Might - y Mount Fu - fu

spit! *Spoken: Ryan: T - T - T - Ti - ki - T - Ti - ki wan na speak-y, speak-y speak-y* *with the might - y spir - it* *Sharpay: So words I will not*

Fu - fu.   T - T - T - mince.   Please make a man _ of my fresh   fish   prince.   This is real

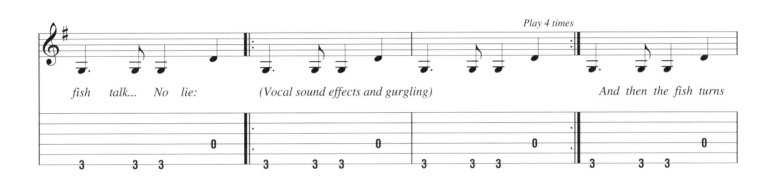

fish   talk... No lie: (Vocal sound effects and gurgling)   And then the fish turns

Play 4 times

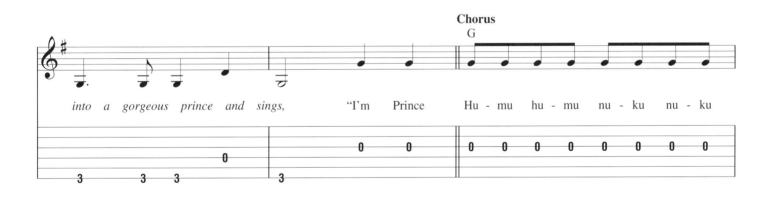

into a gorgeous prince and sings,   "I'm Prince Hu - mu hu - mu nu - ku nu - ku

Chorus
G

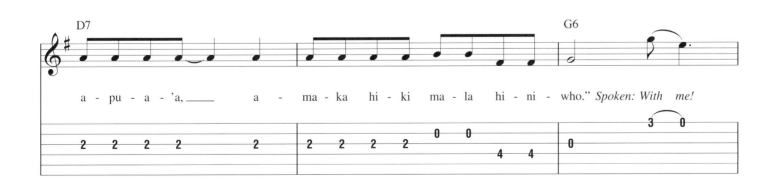

a - pu - a - 'a,___   a - ma - ka hi - ki ma - la hi - ni - who." *Spoken: With me!*

D7   G6

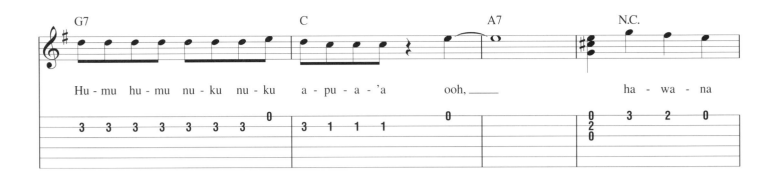

Hu - mu hu - mu nu - ku nu - ku a - pu - a - 'a ooh, _____ ha - wa - na

D.S. al Coda

wa - ka wa - ka wa - ka ni - ki pu pu pu. *Spoken: Everybody!*

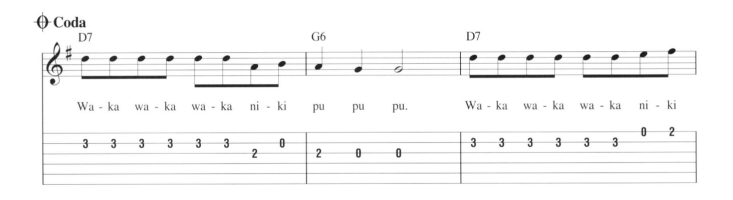

Coda

Wa - ka wa - ka wa - ka ni - ki pu pu pu. Wa - ka wa - ka wa - ka ni - ki

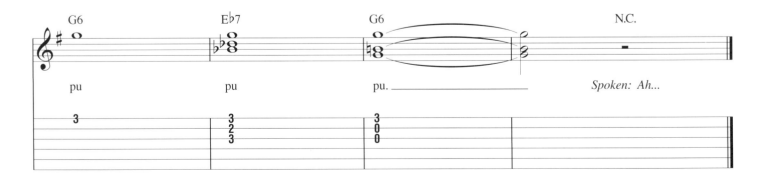

pu pu pu. _____ *Spoken: Ah...*